THE MODERN POETS SERIES   William J. Martz, General Editor

D1328027

THE ACHIEVEMENT OF BROTHER ANTONINUS

A COMPREHENSIVE SELECTION OF HIS POEMS WITH A CRITICAL INTRODUCTION

WILLIAM E. STAFFORD
Lewis and Clark College

SCOTT, FORESMAN AND COMPANY

Photograph of Brother Antoninus on front cover from Wide World Photos.

Pen and ink drawing on back cover by Richard Koppe.

for THOMAS HARDY

Other books in The Modern Poets Series are:

THE ACHIEVEMENT OF THEODORE ROETHKE
THE ACHIEVEMENT OF ROBERT LOWELL

Books by Brother Antoninus

THE RESIDUAL YEARS. New York, New Directions, 1948.
THE CROOKED LINES OF GOD. Detroit, The University of Detroit Press, 1960.
HAZARDS OF HOLINESS. Garden City, New York, Doubleday, 1962.
SINGLE SOURCE. Berkeley, California, Oyez, 1966.
THE ROSE OF SOLITUDE. Garden City, New York, Doubleday, 1967.

CONTENTS

Poems of Struggle and Faith

BROTHER ANTONINUS (WILLIAM O. EVERSON) (1912–   )

William O. Everson was born in 1912 in Sacramento, California. He grew up in Selma, California, where he worked as a farmer and a laborer, and where before World War II he was married. Drafted, he refused military service and was held in conscientious-objector camps, first at Waldport, Oregon, then at Cascade Locks in the same state, and finally at Minersville, California. This interval decisively marked his life, particularly the time spent at Waldport, which was a special camp with a concentration of artists, writers, musicians, and dramatists. Everson played a leading part in the intense and special life in the camps, and at Waldport he published some of his early works, mimeographed on "The Untide Press."

After the war, his marriage broken up, and his kinship with the cultural life around the Bay Area established, he settled in the Berkeley-Oakland area, along with the press, which moved into his backyard.

Publication of *The Residual Years* in 1948 marked his entry into national notice. He received a Guggenheim grant the following year, and since that time he has played one of the leading roles in the "San Francisco Renaissance," with such writers as Kenneth Rexroth and Robert Duncan, who have participated in some of his publishing ventures.

In 1949 William Everson became a Catholic; he worked with the Catholic Worker movement on Skid Row in San Francisco. He became a Dominican brother, Brother Antoninus, and has served since 1951 at St. Albert's College in Oakland, whence he has traveled on many notably successful reading and lecture tours.

BROTHER ANTONINUS—THE WORLD AS A METAPHOR

Racked out in the spread of poetry to follow is one of the most notable, extreme, jagged figures of modern American poetry—the intense, religious, wholly committed *persona* of Brother Antoninus, and his earlier self, the aggressively secular anarchist rebel William Everson. Between these two selves, or aspects of one self, there hums a line of poems held closely along a sustained documentary sequence, portraying, overall, the slow turning of a character under duress:

I speak from a cold heart.
I cry out of a cold climate.
I shake the head of a cold-encrusted man.
I blow a blue breath.
I come from a cold place.
I cry out for another future.
      —"The Blowing of the Seed"

The progression of the sequence is from the young man influenced by his farm background in the California valley:

You cannot shake it, the feeling of mountains, deep in the haze and over
      the cities,
The mass, the piled strength and tumultuous thunder of the peaks.
They are beyond us forever, in fog or storm or the flood of the sun, quiet
      and sure,
Back of this valley like an ancient dream in a man's mind,
That he cannot forget, nor hardly remember,
But it sleeps at the roots of his sight.
      —"Walls"

Through early love and its recollection:

The bruise is not there,
Nor the bullying boy,

1

Nor the girl who gave him the bitter gift,
Under the haws in the hollow dark and the windless air;
But the rue remains,
The rue remains in the delicate echo of what was done;
And he who labors above the lines,
Leans to an ache as old almost
As the howl that shook him in his own birth,
And the heavy blow that beat him to breath
When the womb had widened.

—"The Answer"

Into the clash with the warring state:

And I vow not to wantonly ever take life . . .
And seek to atone in my own soul
What was poured from my past.

—"The Vow"

Coming to adult love:

Under my hand your heart hits like a bird,
Hushed in the palms, a muffled flutter,
And all the instinct of its flight
Shut in its wings.

—"The Blowing of the Seed"

And into announced faith:

The light woke in the windows.
One by one the saints existed,
The swords of their martyrdom healed in their hands.
The linnet opened his voice;
He blistered his throat in the seethe of that rapture.
The suddenness split my skull.

—"A Frost Lay White on California"

2

Pressures in the long development spring from the distinguishing issues of our time—World War II, the moral crises incident to war and the uprootings that go with it, the political turmoil felt by a whole alienated group, and the emotional revulsions of a conscientious and sensitive human being subjected to such pressures. And the solution or resolution, or asserted prospect, hacked out in the poems is most abrupt, emphatic, and extreme. Finally, the unifying element is an announced faith, a religious commitment maintained forcefully in the struggle and sweep of modern challenges.

Those who have found this poetry realize its distinction. But it is not for everyone. For some, it is too disturbing. For all, however, it is phenomenal, a reference point of the modern sensibility.

The poetry of Brother Antoninus confronts the reader with two main hazards, the first an immediate and obvious quality, and the second a more pervasive demand. The immediate quality is that of bleakness and insistent emotional involvement, lying at an extreme from prettiness, and even from recent, more generously updated conceptions of poetry's content. Modern poetry is no valentine, but Brother Antoninus has done more than leave off the lace:

. . . the great elk, caught midway between two scissoring logs,
Arched belly-up and died, the snapped spine
Half torn out of his peeled back, his hind legs
Jerking that gasped convulsion, the kick of spasmed life,
Paunch plowed open, purple entrails
Disgorged from the basketwork ribs
Erupting out, splashed sideways, wrapping him,
Gouted in blood, flecked with the brittle sliver of bone.
                                        —"In All These Acts"

This passage is from a late, religious poem, and in the development of Brother Antoninus' work it seems that the more intense his religious commitment becomes, the more violent the content of his poetry. But even the earliest work has this quality, as a glance at the sequence cited earlier will show: ". . . howl that shook him . . . heavy blow." Even the linnet's song "blistered his throat."

This bleak aspect of the work impressed critics from the first. Kenneth

Rexroth, in an article which helped to launch "the beat generation" into public notice ("San Francisco Letter," in the second issue of *Evergreen Review*), calls William Everson "probably the most profoundly moving and durable poet of the San Francisco Renaissance," and continues: "His work has a gnarled, even tortured honesty, a rugged unliterary diction, a relentless probing and searching, which are not just engaging, but almost overwhelming." And Rexroth goes on to say, "Anything less like the verse of the fashionable literary quarterlies would be hard to imagine." The implication is meant to be honorific: "rugged unliterary diction," not like "the verse of the fashionable quarterlies." But that implication, though understandable, is quite misleading. Rugged as the poems are, they are lavishly literary.

Consider the organization of sound in the following passages. The striking words and pictures may pose as unliterary but are in fact elaborate with repeated sounds and varied, rhymed, slurred progressions:

They came out of the sun with their guns geared,
Saw the soft and easy shape of that island
Laid on the sea,
An unwakening woman,
Its deep hollows and its flowing folds
Veiled in the garland of its morning mists.
                                        —"The Raid"

"No pride!" cried God, "kick me I come back!
Spit on me I eat your spittle!
I crawl on my belly!"
                —"A Frost Lay White on California"

It is clear that the immediate quality of bleakness and shock looms here, but everything is tuned and heightened and artful, even relentlessly artful. Consider the syllables and their sounds, no matter where they come in the lines, no matter how casually they seem to fall—the sun-gun-geared of the first line, the saw-soft, easy-shape of the second line. Think of the hovering erotic implication of the scene in "The Raid." How could you find in any "fashionable quarterly" any verse with more density of repetition than pride-cried-God-kick-come-back? The reader may trust his sense of something special in the language of these poems; they are both rugged *and* literary. The immediate quality of feeling, the shock, derives from something other than just rough words, and in order to identify the cause of the obvious bleakness and shock, we must cast back to the first statement made about the self, the *persona*, which is created out of contrasts.

One kind of poetry—and the poetry of Brother Antoninus is a distinguished example of it—flourishes because it expresses many impulses which practical, politic life coerces most of us to avoid. That is, many of our everyday actions and sayings we adjust to calculations about effects on others; we are purposeful and instrumental with language. But there is another way to live, a way to stay honest without staying silent; and the poetry of Brother Antoninus demonstrates this other way—it is a shock and a delight to break free into the heart's unmanaged impulses. All literature lives in one way or another with this freedom, but the Everson-Antoninus poetry lives openly—even flagrantly—by continual recourse to shock.

Brother Antoninus has committed his whole life to conduct and communication which maintain independence, a stance of accepting what the immediate being can find, and a readiness to reject anything else; he is a passionate romantic. As a radical in politics, as a conscientious objector in war, as a recklessly individual spokesman in his religion, Everson-Antoninus exemplifies to an extreme degree a quality which marks current literature—the exhilaration of rebellion. A reader must accept a certain view if he is to read such a writer sympathetically; he must relish how the literature stiff-arms the genteel, how the author delights in presenting abruptly topics often avoided. Brother Antoninus requires this kind of acceptance immediately and repeatedly.

The shock method is evident in the following passages, chosen from early and late work. Note that the passages do not necessarily prove anything unusual, nor do they have to consist of inherently shocking materials; but each one deliberately confronts the reader with a certain almost electric realization that the writer has shoved against commonly slurred-over or conventionalized human expectations. After an introductory poem, the selection in this text begins with the line: "These verses are lies." Immediately the writer has begun his attack on the reader's expectations. The following demonstrate the prevalence of this *challenge* as a way of writing; the author subjects his reader to a world that hurts:

5

When they rode that hawk-hearted Murietta down in the western hills
They cut the head loose to prove the bounty. . . .
—"Lines for the Last of a Gold Town"

He is a god who smiles blindly,
And hears nothing, and squats faun-mouthed on the wheeling world. . . .
—"Circumstance"

Churchill: the sound of your voice from the eastern air . . . .
Who listen beyond the hammering tongue
For the eloquent fallacy wound at its root
Are not to be wooed. . . .
—"The Unkillable Knowledge"

These are typical passages. They demonstrate the punishing quality in the poems: the reader is to suffer while he receives something that promises an eventual, bitter, satisfying reward.

Bleak, rugged passages, though extreme in the work of Brother Antoninus, and hence an immediate hazard to some readers, do not constitute so much of a barrier as does his other main distinction, the more pervasive quality mentioned earlier. That quality is, bluntly put, didacticism. Brother Antoninus takes a conspicuously unfashionable stand on the issues of belief, assertion, and authority in literature. The results of his stand pervade his poems, which consequently baffle or estrange some readers.

We are accustomed today to accept for the duration of a literary experience all kinds of moral reversals, anti-universes, and ordinarily outrageous assumptions. We ride with the work, accepting the author's most emphatic statements temporarily, without yielding ourselves in any vital way to his assumed authority. We accept his tone as part of the literary experience, but we know that the writer cannot through personal authority coerce our belief. He can only provide us with experiences which we can value for their shimmer and excitement. The fine arts cannot impose; they have to appeal.

However, a generation ago, or longer, an author was a sage, sometimes almost a prophet, a model of some kind. Brother Antoninus is in that tradition, and his poems take on a prophetic, oracular tone. What he presents, he presents as an insight, a truth, not merely as an exercise of the imagination. In his work his voice is direct; he does not turn aside to flirt with fancies and baffling temporary allegiances; there is no Emperor of Ice Cream in his poetry, no Raven saying "Nevermore" to enhance a temporary feeling chosen for literary exercise. Brother Antoninus sets up to be a thinker and guide, a statesman of letters. His stance is that of responsibility. "These verses are lies," yes; but only because they come from a limited intelligence and will, not because the writer is setting out to create passing sensations for the reader.

So the reader of Everson-Antoninus finds himself presented with metaphors intended as truth. The world that is asserted must be linked in its largest events and in its details with a belief that is asserted triumphantly, but then subjected to the terrors and horrors and weaknesses of our existence, and then asserted again. It is the vicissitudes of this faith, surviving in the modern world and in the particulars of the author's life, that have become more and more central in the work of Brother Antoninus.

Even his earlier work is tied to the soul's program of development: his poetry inducted him into his religion, and his religion shapes his poetry. The reader who is unwilling to accept that pattern, who is reluctant to suspend his disbelief in the significance of the particulars of the author's life as the author sees them, will be continually under a strain in reading the poetry; for it asks the reader's participation and makes the author's discoveries into the central rewards of the later poems:

And I crawl.
I will get there.
Like a clubbed snake
I hitch toward freedom.
Out of this skin, this slough,
Across these illusions,
Upon this blood.
　　　—"The Face I Know"

In addition to the evidence in poem after poem that Brother Antoninus is using literature deliberately for purposes other than just the literary, the author himself, outside his poems, declares his objectives. He says in a letter about his work, "I strive for spiritual perfection and make the striving the subject and the themes of my poetry." The Foreword to his 1962 collection, *The Hazards of Holiness*, elaborates:

This is not to say that I despise craftsmanship, but only that the struggle with language is the struggle to make myself comprehensible to myself, to orient my inner and outer being. . . .

Thus I can truthfully say that I have no interest in the conquest of language, as understood by those who seek to achieve a hypostatized aesthetic object. The victories I seek, those of "appeasement and absolution, and something very near to annihilation," are one and all victories over myself, the unremitting attempt to exorcize the demon.

Important as the author's attitude is, and pervasive as its effect is, in the work of Brother Antoninus, the disclaimer of literary ambition need not greatly change the reader's approach. For Brother Antoninus—whatever his explicit intention—is manifestly and even almost helplessly poetic. He maintains creative momentum partly because he continues to be surprised at his own religiousness; he continues to make the kind of visionary statement a discoverer makes. The world says straight to him what it is supposed to say, and for the reader it is the intensity, rather than the validity, of the statements that counts. Almost to the pitch of a Saint Francis, Brother Antoninus encounters the intricate sermons of God acted out by the creatures around us:

Curlews, stilts and scissortails, beachcomber gulls,
Wave-haunters, shore-keepers, rockhead-holders, all cape-top vigilantes,
Now give God praise.
Send up the articulation of your throats
And say His name.
　　　　　　　　　—"A Canticle to the Water Birds"

The rugged shock effect of his writing and the pervasive didactic or moral tone are, then, the most distinctive qualities in the poetry of Brother Antoninus; but two further characteristics—both having to do with the distinctive content of the poetry and both related to the struggle of the self which runs through all the work—may distance for many readers the poems in this text. One characteristic is the extreme alienation modern war has forced on him, and the other is the decidedly personal focus of many of his poems relating to the breakup of a marriage.

In the content of his poetry, and in his life, Brother Antoninus demonstrates forcefully how intense, abrupt, and devastating to the soul modern war is. His distinction in this regard is somewhat blurred by a common supposition that war literature must come from participants, like Wilfred Owen, or Siegfried Sassoon, or Ernest Hemingway; but the young William Everson was even more of a casualty; he did not have even the relative immunity to war which is necessary for reluctant involvement; he did not survive the vision of mass destruction, and was a soul casualty. In common with Robinson Jeffers, who greatly influenced his topics and his style, William Everson saw modern war, from its first flare upon the imagination, as demanding that participants abdicate their humanness; he found himself a spokesman for a kind of being from whom modern warriors cannot be fashioned.

It is difficult to overstate the alienation this writer works from: he gives ordinary readers a view of the place of the absolutist, of the principled rebel. This is not to say that his stance is one of moral superiority; but he has taken the much-contemplated step of saying no to the state, and has been imprisoned for it. That passionate individuality referred to earlier resulted in long-suffering rebellion, in circumstances which continue to test individual values. It is unlikely that many readers even today can participate emotionally, without some qualms, in such a poem as "The Unkillable Knowledge" or, as expressed more simply, in this passage from "The Vow":

I flinch in the guilt of what I am,
Seeing the poised heap of this time
Break like a wave.
And I vow not to wantonly ever take life;
Not in pleasure or sport,
Nor in hate . . .
And seek to atone in my own soul
What was poured from my past. . . .

This pronounced alienation from the "national purpose" when the main group of citizens were mobilized for war has marked one section of our society, and the work of Brother Antoninus is in regard to pacifism probably the most representative of all that the "beat" poets of the San Francisco group have produced. After World War II the Bay Area in

California became a center for many who had been uprooted and had come to know the attractions of the place. Brother Antoninus—then William Everson—had been a prisoner in isolated Civilian Public Service camps during the war years, and he had seen many of his friends taken away to prison. The society around him was alien enough to bring about in-group solidarity among the students, conscientious objectors, and political radicals who began to identify themselves and each other during the postwar years. That background of disaffection with a warring society is worth mention in order to point out that the literary renaissance in San Francisco, as well as later campus and political events of the Bay Area, stems partly from the kind of position exemplified by this poet.

The other markedly distinctive content in what follows comes mostly in the poems about the breaking up of a marriage. One whole section, "The Blowing of the Seed," provides a very ambitious working out of the complex relation between man and woman. They are mutually attracted; they can save each other by the welcome they give to each other's needs. But even that relation carries an implied danger, for all such relations are unstable balances—precarious and disturbing.

Earlier, the poet's "Chronicle of Division" (printed in part here) documents an estrangement between a man and a woman, and something more than a particular estrangement—the poem becomes a religious, psychological drama of attraction and repulsion, complicated by separation enforced by war. So intense are the feelings back of "Chronicle of Division" that some natural image can best serve as a quick indicator; it is convenient to glance at a poem like "Lava Bed" to see how the intensity of vision can reveal itself through the choice of scene and a bitter selecting of components to be held up to view:

Fisted, bitten by blizzards,
Flattened by wind and chewed by all weather
The lava bed lay.
Deer fashioned trails there but no man, ever;
And the fugitive cougars whelped in that lair.
Deep in its waste the buzzards went down to some innominate kill.
The sun fell in it,
And took the whole west down as it died.
Dense as the sea,
Entrenched in its years of unyielding rebuff,
It held to its own.

We looked in against anger,
Beholding that which our cunning had never subdued,
Our power indented,
And only our eyes had traversed.

In this poem a part of the world wonderfully suited for the poet's most fundamental vision is simply held up and described; in appearance, the world is delivering its own meaning by existing in materials and patterns which speak dramatically of struggle, hardness, enduring rebellion. The world is a hard bed, fisted, bitten, flattened, chewed; mankind finds itself confronting that kind of Garden of Eden in the poems of Brother Antoninus. Even when what the world offers has appeal, the greater that appeal, the more poignant its brief existence; and even a poem about childhood allows a quick, strangely erotic glimpse, and then loss:

And what lumps in the throat is the music's magic,
Its exquisite trill,
At the October fairs,
Where the painted horses
Bridled in gold,
Leap up, leap up in that lifeless lope,
With the little girls
Who shriek with joy
And shake out their ribboned hair . . .
And the dream will go. . . .
　　　　　　　　—"The Springing of the Blade"

This bleak view of love, and the forceful stand against war, along with the rugged bluntness of the poems and their uncompromising moral stance—all of these characteristics become pyramided and intensified as Brother Antoninus forces his poems to take upon themselves a big, coherent program—he uses the writing of poetry as a way to master emergencies in his own experience; he *writes his way through* crises and undertakes to wrestle down the ills of our time by means of what he encounters in his development as a poet. All of the poet's encounters are made valid and valued parts of the soul's venture through the world. In recognition of that large purpose, the poems in this text are selected and ordered to help the reader see three main steps in the content of the writer's career. Moreover, it is content that Brother Antoninus talks about when he considers his own work. But before settling for a quick, clear pattern of content, we should emphasize that this poet's technique, his characteristic procedure in writing, also deserves attention.

The "rugged diction" and the shock tactics discussed earlier are like the "personality" of this writer; but his *character* remains for deeper discovery. Note that in the largest, decisive maneuvers of his poems he exercises continuous firm control. He provides constant assurance for the reader, who is guided unswervingly, even as the poem gives the appearance of casual progression. The study of a poem like "The Raid" will demonstrate this constant, assertive control:

They came out of the sun undetected,
Who had lain in the thin ships
All night long on the cold ocean,
Watched Vega down, the Wain hover,
Drank in the weakening dawn their brew,
And sent the lumbering death-laden birds
Level along the decks.

They came out of the sun with their guns geared,
Saw the soft and easy shape of that island
Laid on the sea,
An unwakening woman,
Its deep hollows and its flowing folds
Veiled in the garlands of its morning mists.
Each of them held in his aching eyes the erotic image,
And then tipped down,
In the target's trance,
In the ageless instant of the long ascent,
And saw sweet chaos blossom below,
And felt in that flower the years release.

The perfect achievement.
They went back toward the sun crazy with joy,
Like wild birds weaving,
Drunkenly stunting;
Passed out over the edge of that injured island,

Sought rendezvous on the open sea
Where the ships would be waiting.

None were there.
Neither smoke nor smudge;
Neither spar nor splice nor rolling raft.
Only the wide waiting waste,
That each of them saw with intenser sight
Than he ever had spared it,
Who circled that spot,
The spent gauge caught in its final flutter,
And straggled down on their wavering wings
From the vast sky,
From the endless spaces,
Down at last for the low hover,
And the short quick quench of the sea.

Consider the recurrences in sound and structure, the funnel-shaped action, and the turn signals in this poem:

They came out of the *sun* undetected,
Who *had lain in* the *thin* ships
    . . .
They came out of the sun with their *guns* geared. . . .

The action is in a clear, explicit pattern: they came out . . . they came out . . . and then tipped down . . . they went back . . . at last. . . . The reader knows from the first that the poem is sweeping along toward a definite, summarizable conclusion. Further, the world of this poem is again the typical Antoninus miracle of metaphorical rightness, with war, moral judgment, the erotic images of nature, and final retribution for presumptuous man.

Brother Antoninus' poems are not wandering and exploratory; they drive forward with an assured pattern looming throughout. Consider an early example, "On the Anniversary of the Versailles Peace, 1936." This example typifies the poems; it links to social and political issues; it looks rambling and baggy on the page; it is sustained by the pattern of the natural background, the scene; it subjects the reader to shocks of sensation:

Low is the light;
No red in the sky but a yellow stain;
And that killed snake the sierra all angles and humps on the filled east. . . .

Alliteration recurs throughout this poem; the design is a pattern almost as steady as in Old English verse, with balanced alliterative assertions. And the world spreads itself before the human actors as a delphic lesson:

There is no warring nor fury nor flame, but the hush and the balance;
And one watching can nearly accept with hope that gospel of love which
was Christ's.
But the truce fails; the light spreads, hurling west,
And the sun bursts roaring from the rough hills,
Trampling up the sky, and is free.

Even the alternation between long and short lines adds to the reader's sense of a controlled speaker in these poems. For a time in his development Brother Antoninus shortened his lines, to maximize the kind of come-to-the end-and . . . drop-over effect continually available to the poet, but for the most part he varied the lengths of the lines and thus attained an extreme effect with abruptly bobbed utterances:

I call to mind that violent man who waded the North.
He imagined a slight,
Killed for it;
Made outlaw, lay in the echoing wastes;
Fled to far cities;
Knew dangerous about him the subtle strands of communication
Ticking his doom.
—"The Outlaw"

14

Many of his later poems fill the page from left to right, unloading with detailed care the full reasoning of the writer; but the intermittent short lines continue to mark the style; and often that bobbed line of the early poems turns up again as the ritual intonation of later religious poems:

Now give God praise.
Send up the articulation of your throats,
And say His name.
    —"A Canticle to the Water Birds"

These stylistic distinctions will sustain a reader: the language promises sure advancement through the structure, and the pressured swerve of the lines carries on the assurance.

A further enhancement—so frequent as to become by anticipation a part of the reader's appetite—is intensity as communicated by strains and displacements in the language. For instance, often scenes or actions become illuminated for the reader by a word or phrase which indicates immediate technical involvement on the part of the speaker, a flashing out with terms used by adepts—a crane waits to "gig" fish; or a small bird, "the swart junket," "skits" in the thicket; a river "cuts" its way to the sea. Events come into the consciousness with immediacy, signaled in and accommodated by a writer who feels his closeness to the action.

Sometimes this effect of closeness derives from forcing the language to accept adjustments which appear to be necessary because of emergencies in stating something felt too distinctly for communication in ordinary language: a noun may be forced to become a verb, for instance. At times this procedure is like a mannerism, though it always creates an intensity:

All gone, all broken,
Smashed and smithereened. . . .
Speak from the bloodied past, the failed venture.
    —"The Blowing of the Seed"

The effect of this custom-made wording is to induce in the reader a realization of tension. The poems are never allowed to become inert, are never standard formulations. The effort of the self to attain its place, its soul's rescue, is reflected in the effort of the poems to attain the resolution intimated by their apparent strain. In effect, the poems act out, even in the details of their wording, the whole effort intimated from the first of this discussion, the progression of Everson to Antoninus, the evolution of the *persona* animating the successive poems.

Strangely, it is this very feeling of effort that has led some critics to assume that the fox is not cunning. Whether cunning is the right word or not, an examination of Brother Antoninus' work will certainly show that he treats the language with that same confidence and control which distinguishes the work of the most elaborately "literary" writer.

One other distinction in the style of this poet deserves recording here: he has carried all of his force and individuality into public readings; and again he qualifies as an important representative of the San Francisco group of poets in that he has helped to establish poetry reading in its current popularity, through many readings locally and in a number of trips across the country. His appearances are striking. He is tall, and though he appears to understate his posture, he is still tall. In the long robe of the Dominican, he dramatizes his stance. He adjusts to different audiences, apparently finding his manner as he goes along, but the effect is always that his poems appear to come from a need to communicate directly; in the reading as in the writing, a personal message dominates. His voice is piercing, a reed instrument. And he intones and invokes as he moves about the stage. He has confidence in his poems, and he is capable of putting the audience under a strain as they have to wait for him to begin. He challenges and taunts. He jolts and teases the audience. As he writes for purposes larger than the literary, so he reads with apparent intention of using poems for changing the lives of his hearers.

Directly using poems for the sake of his hearers, as part of his life applied to the immediate situation, is typical of the career of Brother Antoninus: he has carried from farm to camp to home to monastery the accumulation of his work and even the means to print it. As he himself was a printer and as his friends were often engaged in writing and publishing, and as they often considered their work to be independent, outside the mainstream, his bibliography has become very much tangled. His writing and publishing make an elaborate puzzle, with partial printings of certain large works, and with consequent gaps in the material he considers continuous. The selection presented herewith weaves as best it can with a range of work from the earliest to the latest in book publication; and the sequence draws into itself material not yet in book form. The acknowledgments page will enable a reader to trace some of the main strands of the bibliographical puzzle, but because the line of his development lends itself to certain simplified clarifications, it has been thought best to group the poems into the three imposed sections indicated in the Contents, and to offer a somewhat elaborated explanation here.

Each section marks a stage in chronology identified by a phrase which to a fair degree indicates a stage in the poet's development. In the later 1930's and into the 1940's, while the writer was farm worker, student, and then prisoner in a camp for conscientious objectors, he was writing what he has classed as poems of "the natural imagination," that is, poems which rely for their value on sense impressions as guides for the self. He was at this time much influenced by Robinson Jeffers. Though always alerted to overtones in natural experience, William Everson, before his change of religion and name, was not identified with any church. In fact, some of his poems from the conscientious-objector camps accurately depict a certain distance he maintained from the professedly religious objectors; in particular, the sequence called "Chronicle of Division" reveals that distance and some traces of rebellion against the program accepted by "conformers" in the camps:

The newcomer marvels,
Beholding about him wherever he enters,
The direct head,
The declarative face,
That wears its look like an open hand.
. . .
Till time taught him less,
Revealing the brittle bias
The unseen error that makes human the saint. . . .

His official listing in the directory of the camps identifies him as a "farmer, poet, printer," and his religion is listed, "none."

Overlapping the first period and extending into the 1950's, was a period here labeled that of "metaphysical search." This term merely serves to identify poems which appear to move from confusion and discouragement and social indictment toward some achieved sense of direction. This division is probably the most schematic and least valid, chronologically, of the three divisions offered here for the convenience of the reader. The difficulty of achieving helpful groupings is apparent from the date appended to "The Vow," which ends this section. That date is 1940, but no later poem more appropriately takes up into itself the scene, the sense of direction, and the religious overtone later to become predominant:

Delicate and soft,
The grass flows on the curling palms of my hands.
The gophers under the ground
Fashion their nests in the cool soil.
I lift up my eyes,
And they find the bearing that swings the sky,
And I turn toward home,
Who have gathered such strength as is mine.

The last section, representing the current stage in this poet's development, contains the Roman Catholic religious poems. They celebrate, beyond the detailed suffering, a security—a continuing struggle but in some respects a resolution of the author's long struggle to achieve a coherent self. The poems hammer a direct, religious view, and they even approximate ritual patterns at times; but they do not mark a complete change from the tone and technique of the earlier work: the writer has brought his metaphors, and his general sense of the world as a metaphor, into the frame for repeated assertion of his Roman Catholic faith. He has found it possible to view himself as one of the "crooked lines" with which God writes straight.

William E. Stafford

Let breath keep to the lung.
She'd never believe,
Had soul for her sung,
Mind gonged, or the bell heart rung.

5 Not one tongue-tolling word
Would she believe,
Though high court heard,
Sealed the assent, and the State averred.

What deficit at birth
10 Blinded her eye?
What scant, what dearth
Blanks out her own, her immeasurable worth?
(This passage introduces Part II
of *The Residual Years*)

OUTSIDE THIS MUSIC

These verses are lies.
Who bends the hard hand over the lines,
Shaping the words, feeling the gust of an ancient mood
Blow through the room, the weight of the night and the broken hills,
5 Hammers no truth.

He feels up through the floor the strength that is cramped in the stone
of the earth
Push at his flesh; the lips stammer on darkness.
Into the delicate substance of the blood
Flows the long wind, deep drives the night.
10 The eyes will be blind, the throat shattered and mute
In the wave of thunder of the fallen sky.

What lies outside the closed and hollow music of this verse
Runs in the earth, in the plunge of the sun on the summer sky.
There is wind on the walls,
15 And the feeling of tough wild weeds straining all outdoors,
And the bruised mouth, forming the shape of a word,
Turning toward night.

TRIFLES

The man laughing on the steep hill tripped on a stone,
Fell broken among boulders, suffered his life out under the noon sun.
The young wife, when the tire blew on the Trimmer road,
Took that long crash screaming into the rocks.
5 By sand slipping, by the shoe splitting on the narrow street,
By the parting of atoms,
By the shaping of all those enormous trifles we plunge to that border,
Writhing under the long dark in the agony of destruction,
The great sky and the flaming west riding our eyes,
10 Gathering in from the heavy hills, and the tides of the sea.

O poets! sleepers forever under the soil!
You have spoken it out of the bitter mouths hundreds of times,
Your anguish beats from the pages, beats on our bored and indolent
sight!
But earth yields and a man is smothered,
15 Wood splits and a man is broken—
Simply, the mute and terrible ease of the function—
And you and your shouting burst up before us,
We taste that wry and sterile bitterness,
And pound with our hands on the dark.

LINES FOR THE LAST OF A GOLD TOWN

MILLERTON, CALIFORNIA. 1936

When they rode that hawk-hearted Murietta down in the western hills
They cut the head loose to prove the bounty,
And carried it here to this slope on the river's rim
Where the town sprawled, but no longer.
5 In a jar on the courthouse desk it lay for days,
While the wide-wheeled wagons swam in the dust,
And the word ran: up-state and down the folk heard it and sang;
And the head in the jug on the Millerton desk
Sneered through the glass at the faces.

10 Now the thick grass.
The willow fringe on the water's edge drinks the March sun and has
peace,
Takes the deep sky, and bird-singing, the low mottled music, but heavy
with peace.
On the low slope over the stream, with the roof of it thin and the win-
dows gone,
The old courthouse alone on the meadow squats in the drag of the years:
15 Musty, floors fallen, the smell of dead time on it,
Of the killed moment, the stifling accumulation of sheer existence
Thick in the air and the wind takes it.

There can be heard over the earth,
Running in deep and vibrant gusts, the broken music;
20 Blowing, the reverberation of uttered sound,
Of bawd's talk and squaw's talk and the male-throated laughter,
Primal and harsh and brutely intense.
The mind's eye fashions the picture: glare on the night and the shacks
crowded,
The congestion of flesh, of reeking animal flesh; blood burning, nerves
blazing.

25 And one turns to the years,
Through the soft disintegration, thinking:
Where are the seekers and where are the whores?
What has come of the roaring, the lewd language, the riotous lusts and
the acts?—
Here, where are only slow trees and the grass,
30 And this empty hulk and symbol of an order jeered at,
Spat at, hooted and scorned in the days of its birth!

Crumbles, the leaf; sags, the used stalk;
Softly, the alteration, the touch.
It has been said, often, tongues hating it.
35 It has been said.

ON THE ANNIVERSARY OF THE VERSAILLES PEACE, 1936

Low is the light;
No red in the sky but a yellow stain;
And that killed snake the sierra all angles and humps on the filled east.
In the low fields where no song is and the wind dead,
5 The forces are caught, the wrestlers hang in the wide sky, blended and
still;
There is no warring nor fury nor flame, but the hush and the balance;
And one watching can nearly accept with hope that gospel of love which
was Christ's.
But the truce fails; the light spreads, hurling west,
And the sun bursts roaring from the rough hills,
10 Trampling up sky, and is free.

Cry peace! if you will.
There is in the plasm the mood that denies it.
There is in the fist the love of the striking,
And out of the heart the savage inviolate flame.
15 Life comes to it shining: grass choking, the wolves slashing.
Napoleon, nor Caesar, nor Genghis could have led the hordes,
Unwilling, into the jaws. They ran down singing.
And I who hold the poor dream as passionately as any,
Expect it never. We have sprung from the loins of that mother, the past,
20 And got something but love from her dugs.

NOON

The wind down, hushed;
In the sudden suspension of time and all motion
The sun lies heavily on the hand;
Spreads on the tilting cheek;
5 The ocean of light that is widest at noontime
Swells on the mind

24

And no leaf turning, no flag for the restless eye,
The heart takes softly unto itself
Some deep and voluptuous meaning;
10 And filling, it flows to the blood like sleep in the veins,
And the thick light floats on the shoulders.

Deep sun, deep sky;
No wind now for the dance of the leaves;
But the light clean on the shape of the neck;
15 And the deep sound of the heart.

CIRCUMSTANCE

He is a god who smiles blindly,
And hears nothing, and squats faun-mouthed on the wheeling world,
Touching right and left with infinite lightning-like gestures.
He is the one to pray to, but he hears not, nor sees.

5 Because the man who is my father chanced to a certain town in a cer-
tain state,
And met the woman, my mother, and met her again in another place,
and they loved and were wed;
Because the night she conceived, one sperm and not another, of all that
he gave her, touched home and developed,
I am tall, not short; and dark, not blond; and given to indolence and
dreaming.
Because it happened like that through the line of my fathers—
10 (A meeting here, a touching there,
Back through what shrouded and imponderable journeys of time)
This shape of my life the inexorable brood of those ages of chance,
And I at the peak: every move that I make to pattern the form of what's
off and beyond.

He is the god to pray to; he sits with his faun's mouth and touches the
world with hovering hands.
15 He is the god—but he sees not, nor hears.

WALLS

East, the shut sky:
Those walls of the mountains hold sunrise and wind under their backs.
If you tread all day vineyard or orchard,
Or move in the weather on the brimming ditch,
5 Or throw grain, or scythe it down in the early heat,
Taken by flatness, your eye loving the long stretch and the good level,
You cannot shake it, the feeling of mountains, deep in the haze and over
the cities,
The mass, the piled strength and tumultuous thunder of the peaks.
They are beyond us forever, in fog or storm or the flood of the sun, quiet
and sure,
10 Back of this valley like an ancient dream in a man's mind,
That he cannot forget, nor hardly remember,
But it sleeps at the roots of his sight.

THE STRANGER

Pity this girl.
At callow sixteen,
Glib in the press of rapt companions,
She bruits her smatter,
5 Her bed-lore brag.
She prattles the lip-learned, light-love list.
In the new itch and squirm of sex,
How can she foresee?

How can she foresee the thick stranger,
10 Over the hills from Omaha,
Who will break her across a hired bed,
Open the loins,
Rive the breach,
And set the foetus wailing within the womb,
15 To hunch toward the knowledge of its disease,
And shamble down time to doomsday?

THE ANSWER

The bruise is not there,
Nor the bullying boy,
Nor the girl who gave him the bitter gift,
Under the haws in the hollow dark and the windless air;
5 But the rue remains,
The rue remains in the delicate echo of what was done;
And he who labors above the lines,
Leans to an ache as old almost
As the howl that shook him in his own birth,
10 As the heavy blow that beat him to breath
When the womb had widened.

For boyhood bent him:
Awkward at games he limped in the offing.
Youth yoked him:
15 The tyrannous sex trenchant between his flowering limbs,
Nor strength to subdue it.
Now manhood makes known the weaknesses flawed in the emergent
soul:
Guilt marring the vision,
The whimpering lusts and the idiot rages.

20 And the years gnaw at him.
Deep to the dawns does he marshal all skill at the intractable page,
But nothing converges;
Grown pudgy with time he takes blow and rebuff,
Is baffled,
25 Hugs to the rind of his crumpled pride,
Endures only out of an obscure persistence
Grained in his soul.

But at last comes a time, when, triggered by some inconsequent word,
The breath of an odor,
30 Some casual touch awakening deep in the somnolent flesh
Its ancient response,
The inner locks open;
And clear down its depth,
The delicate structure of that rue harvest
35 Trembles to life.
The thought stirs in its seed;
The images flower;
Sucked from their secret recesses of mind
The shadowy traces of all intuition float into being,
40 And the poem emerges,
Freighted with judgment,
Swung out of the possible into the actual,
As one man's insight matches mankind's at the midpoint of language,
And the meeting minds reduplicate in the running vowel
45 Their common concern.

Then here rides his triumph:
Caught in his doom he had only his anguish,
But the human pattern imposes across his stammering mind
Its correctional hand.
50 What was vague becomes strict;
What was personal blooms in the amplification of art;
And the race pronounces;
Out of his mouth there issues the judgment of all mankind,
And he touches attainment in that.

THE FRIENDS

They had spoken for years,
Meeting at times in the late cafes,
Chancing together on the hosted street,
A passing word.
5 Over the casual cups of coffee,
In the years' flux,
In the seasons' motion,
Their friendship deepened;
And one fog-folded night,
10 Seeing her home through the emptying ways,
The slow concatenation of time
Turned at the out-post of her porch,
And he did not go.

The room breathed of her presence.
15 Undressing beside her,
In the high mounting of his perception,
He had the sense of total conjunction
With all that she was.
He watched the well-tempered body divesting its sheaths,
20 Saw the sculptural back,
Knew the flare of the hips from the waist's weal,
And the hair-darkened hollow,
Where all the body's inleading lines
Sucked toward center.
25 She made no evasion.
The cup they had carried so long atremble
They let pour over,
Drench downward,
And such the reciprocal nature of trust,
30 They could beg no lack.

For time sustained them.
The subtle progression of minute means
Rose now in its recapitulation,
Enriching the present,
35 Yielding it amplitude and scope,
Providing out of its vast reserve
Its bountiful wealth.
Having fashioned the present out of the past,
The past and its promise achieved fulfillment.
40 They endured no regression,
Who knew even in this,
The tidal dark, the volcanic night,
The rash eruptive rush of the blood,
The discriminate mind makes its choices.

THE ILLUSION

The low wind talks on the boards of the house,
Gains and recedes, night deepens.
And feeling it round you,
The touch of this peace on your full spirit,
5 You know the illusion: men in the world stronger than you
Bleeding under the roofs, falling under the wheels,
Pitching down from the sky to lie in the fields under blunt stars;
Hear in the night the long wail
Calling the cars to some roadside shambles;
10 Remember him who lay on the mountain,
Holding his shattered foot, and the axe;
Think of the torn mouths begging release down the groove of the years;
Sit in your peace, drinking your ease in a quiet room,
Soft in your dreams—and the men falling.

15 The cities are shining.
The great ships west in the welter of seas
Hunt out the islands.
You feel the high impregnable ranges of earth leaning in darkness.
You feel the texture of your living flesh
20 Soft on the bone.

You rest in your peace.
They pitch and go down with the blood on their lips,
With the blood on the broken curve of their throats,
With their eyes begging.

25 You rest in the ease and fortune of your dreams, and they break.
In the solitary towns, on the long roads high in the folded hills
The night blows over them rushing and loud, and they fall.

THE HARE: AN EARLIER EPISODE

The hare running for life in the sparse growth
Broke cover,
His ears low and his legs driving,
But sure blew the shot,
5 And shattered and mauled he thrashed in the rubble,
His entrails sprawling the red ruck,
And those angered ants at their work.

Then surely that time
Evil hooded my heart;
10 Surely that time
The source of all hurt and harm and heavy woe
Pinioned me high in the frozen air,
Gazing far down the blue height of my indifference,
My ears stoppered against those piteous cries
15 That swam up about me,
My stone eyes cold in my iron face,
The central terror and the separate hurt
Far at my feet.

Between that time and this
20 The subtle and transigent forces of growth

Have altered my mind,
Nor can I now say the way that it was,
But ice thawed,
Height dwindled,
25 The dwindling height threw me racked on the ground by that bleeding
hare,
My torn flesh and my splintered bone
Tangled with his.

Against the frozen impossible fact of redemption,
(No act undone,
30 The hare mewling and jerking
Down time from now on)
I draw all my strength,
And wear as I can the measure of pity,
The meed of forbearance,
35 And the temperance fathered of guilt.

THE RESIDUAL YEARS

As long as we looked lay the low country.
As long as we looked
Were the ranchos miled in their open acres,
The populous oaks and the weedy weirs.
5 There were birds in the rushes.

And deep in the grass stood the silent cattle.
And all about us the leveled light.
Roads bent to the bogs;
Fenced from the fields they wound in the marshes.
10 We saw slim-legged horses.

We saw time in the air.
We saw indeed to the held heart of an older order,
That neither our past nor that of our fathers
Knew part in the forming,
15 An expansive mode remarked through the waste of residual years,
Large in its outline,
Turning up from its depth these traces and wisps
That hung yet on through a cultural close
We had thought too faint to recapture.

THE OUTLAW

I call to mind that violent man who waded the North.
He imagined a slight,
Killed for it;
Made outlaw, lay in the echoing waste;
5 Fled to far cities;
Knew dangerous about him the subtle strands of communication
Ticking his doom.
Cornered at last he knelt in the night
And drew like magnet the metal loosed in the acrid air.

10 And so went down.
Nor ever knew that what brought him such bounty
Was only the wearing out of a way—
He and the wolves and the dazed tribes
Numb in their dissolution.
15 Blind in their past,
The past betrayed them;
The trees of tradition screened from their sight
The enormous forest of the waiting world—
As we, we also, bound in our patterns,
20 Sense but see not the vestigial usages grooving our lives.
Like some latter-day outlaw we crouch in our rooms,
Facing the door and the massed future,
And draw doom down on our heads.

THE REVOLUTIONIST

His enemies learned.
In the small of the nights,
In the pre-dawn chill of the swart streets,
What once they despised
5 He taught them to dread.
The smouldering eye in the iron face
Marked many a man.
He wore the zealot's heart,
And such was his gift
10 Power poured to his use.

But his enemies learned.
At cost, with error,
They bled, but they learned.
Learned late, but learned well;
15 Learned, indeed, only at last,
But learned in time;
And they too mustered;
They too mastered the means of the small hours,
His stratagems, his known deceits.

20 He made over the roofs,
Half-naked and injured;
Skulked by day in the hedges,
The intrepid face glaring out from the stones with a beast's bale;
Traveled by night the desolate lanes;
25 Crossed with the moon the hostile border;
Wandered for weeks;
Found far haven.

For a time he aspired.
Men remembered his terrible face,
30 And plotted his triumph.
They were hunted down.
Under that fierce remorseless bane his cause withered.
He grew old in time,
Subsisting on scraps in a bleak room,
35 Hating about him the foreign tongues, the foreign faces.

Fixed in his thwartion,
Like some banished lord,
Like Bonaparte, sick for his sovereignty,
The wind of whose want
40 Poured out of the waste of the South Atlantic
Toward France and fulfillment,
He fastened the past within his grinding heart,
And eked out his life on its gall.

THE UNKILLABLE KNOWLEDGE

Churchill: the sound of your voice from the eastern air,
Borne on the singing lanes of the sky,
And caught in this room.

What we hear: the old imperious English speech,
5 That out of its wealth and its rich evocation,
And out of the singular English past,
Broaches the heritage
Boned in the structure of our common lives.
Your terrible warning and your crying appeal
10 Blow through the mind.
We suddenly see in its vast implication,
The leveling of London,
And the implacable voice
Speaks on in its rigor,
15 Speaks on in its need,
And breeds of that need the slow indignation,
The rock-rooted anger that fosters resolve.

But draw as you do on all the right,
It yet is not yours;

20 Though with blood you bind it,
Not yet is it yours.

For even beyond your tenor of soul,
Beyond your courage, your strength, your incomparable speech,
Resides a morality deeper than any your cause may claim,
25 An insight sheer through the animal manifestations of terror and rage,
Beyond nation, the divisions of race,
The smouldering heritage of hate,
To coil at last at the final unkillable knowledge
That lives among men.

30 Shout down the sky.
Who listen beyond the hammering tongue
For the eloquent fallacy wound at its root
Are not to be wooed.
Drawing all the detail to one iron focus
35 They watch with eyes wide;
And they wait.

Spring, 1941

THE APPROACH

Breaking back from the sea we ran through low hills,
The long deserted pavement falling and winding,
Lonesome farms in their locked valleys,
The coastal range, ancient even as mountains,
5 Moulded by wind.

Till inland we curved to the far converging city,
Seeing it laid at the hill's heel,
Whirlpooled, the long lines of its power,
Beacons for planes revolving the dusk,
10 The black trails of concrete slipping down grade
To the first clusters, to the city,
Thick in the gloom with its few lights showing,
With its veils, its myriad roofs,
And its heavy pounding heart.

THE VOW

The sky darkens;
Lights of the valley show one by one;
The moon, swollen and raw in its last quarter,
Looks over the edge;
5 And I kneel in the grass,
In the sere, the autumn-blasted,
And seek in myself the measure of peace
I know is not there.

For now in the east
10 The flyers high on the rising rivers of air
Peer down the dark,
See under the flares the red map of the ruined town,
Loose cargo, turn,
And like north-hungry geese in the lifting spring
15 Seek out the long way home.

The low freighters at sea
Take in their sides the nuzzling dolphins that are their death,
Burst and go under;
Their crews lie on the rafts in the deep fogs,
20 And will not be found,
And will starve at last on the blue waste.

And I dream the delusion of men twisting in death
Without honor or love;
I feel the unresolvable tension forming within me,
25 Knowing myself of the same breed,
And I shatter the hollow weeds.

For yet in my blood are Leif the Lucky,
And Thald, and Snorre, and that fierce old man
Who fought all day in the walls,
30 Going down at last with his throat pierced,
His great beard bloody and stiff.

There are the stunned eyes and the gibbering mouths,
Those who endured crazy with hate,
And who bore in their loins the warped seed
35 That never forgot.

I, the living heir of the bloodiest men of all Europe;
And the knowledge of past tears through my flesh;
I flinch in the guilt of what I am,
Seeing the poised heap of this time
40 Break like a wave.

And I vow not to wantonly ever take life;
Not in pleasure or sport,
Nor in hate,
Nor in the careless acts of my strength
45 Level beetle or beast;
And seek to atone in my own soul
What was poured from my past;
And bear its pain;
And out of the knowledge of dissolution
50 Bring my pity and bring my ruth. regret / compassion

Delicate and soft,
The grass flows on the curling palms of my hands.
The gophers under the ground
Fashion their nests in the cool soil.
55 I lift up my eyes,
And they find the bearing that swings the sky,
And I turn toward home,
Who have gathered such strength as is mine.

Autumn, 1940

from CHRONICLE OF DIVISION

III

This, then, is our world.
Having entered the gate
Who is there to measure the length we will stay?
The factors that manage that endurance have yet to be formed.
5 This much we know:
Blood will be poured.
The world in constriction must loosen, unlock,
The tides withdraw,
And all the wide chaos,
10 That dwarfs our meager participation,
Must have its great way.
Yet the impassive calendar governs our minds.
And the gate remains,
Broad for departure,
15 To pass if we choose.
Some of us do,
Openly asking the consequent hurt,
Or by stealth and deceit in the moon's blindness.
Only rumor returns.
20 We others remain,
Holding within us the vast temptation and the obscure threat,
And nurse the wide cleavage of will.

IV

The newcomer marvels,
Beholding about him wherever he enters,
25 The direct head,
The declarative face,
That wears its look like an open hand.

For him in his newness,
Fresh from the world,
30 No bitterness breeds,
None slander,
None thieve,
None rail in anger nor smoulder in hate;
But the abundant leaven engendered of trust,
35 Earns of itself its reciprocal usage,
And endures no abuse.

This he had dreamed,
In his glimmering visions,
Projecting the shape of some nebulous life—
40 And here he would hold it,
Till time taught him less,
Revealing the brittle bias,
The unseen error that makes human the saint,
Thwarts the idealist,
45 Marks the martyr,
For none is immune.
What the soul strives for is not to be had.
That too would he learn.
But here for a time it is true.

V

50 The pacifist speaks,
Face to face with his own kind,
And seeks to fashion a common course
That all may mark.
But whatever he offers,
55 Finds already framed in another's thought
A divergent approach.
The binding belief that each allows
Is cruxed on rejection:
Thou shalt not kill.

60 But for all the rest,
   What Voice shall speak from the burning bush,
   In the work-site noons,
   When the loaf is broken,
   And brief and rebuttal countercross,
65 And no one wins?

   Apart on his rock,
   The forester sucks his sufficient quid,
   And never hears,
   At one with the landscape,
70 That crouches behind its masked firs,
   Its skeletal snags,
   Brooding upon the lost myth
   Created once in its unfathomable past
   And never regained—
75 But it wants to,
   It waits, it waits,
   Its immense obsession—

   And when speech runs out,
   When the rebel lays down his irksome axe at last,
80 And takes his stand,
   The crude pencil,
   Moistened with spit and tobacco juice,
   Has only to scrawl the offending name,
   And the man and his reasons
85 Converge toward those walls at the world's end
   Where all questions die.

from THE SPRINGING OF THE BLADE

But when the blade was sprung up,
and brought forth fruit,
then appeared the tares also.

PART ONE: TIME OF YEAR
    The Iron Dimension
It wears.
Even the young perceive it.
Even the infant,
5 Before he hardly has any perspective,
Moves with a wakeful wide-eyed caution
Into time's change.
That house-law he lives by:
Discovers one day its true substance,
10 A mere rule.

But will cross in that testing to the inviolate region,
The true absolute of human pain,
Entered with some injurious act
That can't be forgiven and will never be forgot,
15 The hurt and the hurter
Strung in the iron dimension,
Fixed there forever.

In our town, when I was a boy,
A man ran off with a grass widow,
20 "A woman of good looks and loose morals",
Left to his wife
Only the children and a galled pride.
What the father was she blocked from their minds,
An exorcism of silence.
25 The eldest, grown out of girlhood,
Kept a suitor for eight years before she decided.
They were to marry in June;
In April the woman
Caught them together on the parlor sofa
30 In the naked act.

She came to my mother;
I heard from the near room;
Her sobs shook through the house:
"Why couldn't they wait!"
35 Over and over, choked in the wet kerchief,
"Why couldn't they wait!"

It is hard to wait,
In the drab parlor under the drapes,
Under the faded pictures and the papered walls,
40 The stained and papered years . . .

But that does not redeem.
In the woman's heart, the old mother,
There that terrible cry burst with its burden,
To see the sin
45 Substantiate in the reckless act;
And the lip that never trembled in public,
Sustained in pride while the lean years grated,
That lip broke,
And the stringy throat gave its giant grief,
50 That splits, and, like the wolf's howl on the winter crag,
Shivers the over-hanging snow
To start its crumble, its monstrous slide.

But no. Nor the blind hurt
Ran out no brutal, bloody course.
55 They made their marriage;
In proper season blessed with a babe.

But that does not redeem.
Not there, in the old woman's heart,
However she came to dandle that child.
60 For the taint, like a birthmark laid on a baby's face,
The delineament of an ancient lust
Spied out in the dimple—
And what caught in her throat,
Revulsion and shame and the gagging pride
65 In a raw mingle . . .

She went under the clay
Her jawbone clenched on the obstinate
Unobliterable, not-to-be-swallowed
Gorge of reproof:
70 A sharp stone in a chicken's craw,
Stuck there forever.

ODOR OF AUTUMN

And in the cooling weather,
Over the canyons,
Over the sun-invested slopes,
75 That hold, like tawny wine, all summer's hauteur;
Over the hazy draws and the pine-thicket knolls,
Drifts the unmistakable odor of autumn.

And I am reminded
That once more now it is the season of school;
80 And on country lanes
Again the school children make their way,
Wearing that openness about the eyes
Where fields have glimmered,
And the ground-squirrel pierced his skirling note;
85 Bearing about them a something restless,
Something unruly,
The charge of freedom,
Nature's benign tolerance,
That will in time be curbed, made docile,
90 Smoothed as the tousled hair
Before the glass is smoothed and parted;
Sent with them off down the road
To an anxious future that long ago
Lost what they cannot keep.

THE CARROUSEL

95 For the child,
In love with looking,
The world goes wide to his earthly gaze
And there is no past.
The round eye,
100 That stares at dusk from the dark hill,
And sees the moon in the tree,
Rough hands on its face,
Fills then to overflowing
With autumn's wonder,
105 Not knowing what the cold means,
But that the moths are gone.

And what lumps in the throat is the music's magic,
Its exquisite trill,
At the October fairs,
110 Where the painted horses
Bridled in gold,
Leap up, leap up in that lifeless lope,
With the little girls
Who shriek with joy
115 And shake out their ribboned hair.

It will be years, years.

And the dream will go,
Will keep only the trace,
As of a forgotten fondness,
120 Wholly lived out in youth's maturation,
But caught now, over the boardwalk,
Just for a moment,
Drifting across the summer music,
Where the carrousel tinkles and whirls.

125 But out there the sea,
 That has been hushed and torpid,
 Half asleep under a squat moon,
 Scruffs up its strength,
 And all the intervening years
130 Crack in two.

THE AREAS OF CORRUPTION

 And the years reveal.
 And there comes a time when,
 Waking out of a walking dream,
 As the child, each day, wakes with a wonder in its eye,
135 He rouses up the recumbent head
 To a knowledge of the past.

 And perhaps it is that the splendor of a tree,
 Leafing the curb near the suburban mansions,
 In the suggestible season,
140 Will make a meaning of itself;
 Will write its own articulation in the cooling of the air;
 Will say, with the loosing of its leaf,
 All he could say,
 Who looks by the marigold, loitering,
145 His slow shoe scuffing the gravel.

 And the pipe-stem, like the chewn twig of his boyhood,
 And the jack-knife clasped near his knuckle,
 Can these be touched,
 Or what lies in them,
150 That somethingness,
 Like a sleep on them,
 As if the years had placed them there,
 With their special substance,
 To be at hand when the leaf fell,
155 And lead him back?

46

The sun says, Yes, it is true,
It is the sameness of the light,
It leaned so then.
The bird in the hawthorn,
160 Near his foot, says it,
Its head cocked in the known way,
The assurance of its eye.
And the lady, so smartly clad,
Whose heel on the flagstone,
165 In its luxurious clip, confirms it,
And whose glance, behind the flecked veil,
Bestows its fleeting speculation—
Is she not the same, the very same,
Who leaned above the little head,
170 Touched him, left him laved and swimming
In the lambent smile?

He cannot turn.
The heel-note clips away, smartly,
Out of the clinging clamorous ear
175 It trips and vanishes, its brief note
Gone like a flashing smile
That left its beckon but would not wait,
Lost beyond the hedges,
Where only an old gardener,
180 Seamed and serious,
Pokes among the shrubs.

The substance of the years,
Their very texture.
Like the milkweed down,
185 That drifts with the drifting air,
This time of year,
On the roadsides at home.
Or as the cat-tail
Lays out its fluff on the placid water
190 In the dryness of the fall,
Before the rains come in.
The very substance.

Gone with the autumns,
Washed out under a leaching rain;
195 Gone with the mother's mouldering smile;
With the father's frown
Stained in the earth.
Gone where the schoolmates of the past
Have long since gone,
200 To their separate lives,
Only the echo of their shouts
Caught in the scrappage of a phrase,
Where that cry persists,
Plaintive and long,
205 Calling him out to the leaf-frolic game,
Before the dark sets in.

And the areas of all corruption
Cockle and fray in the torn heart.
The foxed pages rattle in an unrelenting wind.
210 And the written word
Blurs, fades as the sight itself,
Worn out with looking,
Fades in the face,
When the eighty year's infant,
215 Witless and daft,
Wholly resumes his past.

PART TWO: THERE WILL BE HARVEST

Thus in these ways, these glimpsings back,
Do I call up the days of my childness.
Thus in these nights I muse at work. . . .

220 At Treesbank, turned autumn, came one,
Bird-lover, learned in their ways.
From our low-roofed porch
He hooted the owls up to the house,
In closest dusk, when cypress
225 Gathered up gloom the orchard had engendered.
What quavered in the trees
We could not see, but the soft spokenness,
The mutability between those three,
The mated birds, the muted man,
230 Holding their whispered concourse.

There too at sundown, south,
Saw how the sea-pregnated fog
Crossed on the holding hills.
Eastward it shot its long advancing column,
235 Always, laying across that portion of the coast
Its deep dimension. Then dark drew down;
We finished chores
Soon under prickling stars, dined fully,
Forgetful of that widened world
240 That all day long absorbed us.
But later, outside, a trip for stovewood,
Saw how the fog had come, with darkness,
Filling the creekbeds, taking the slope,
Up through the orchard, a soft coming,
245 A gentle drawing in. There was no noise.
The eye cast up still swept on stars.
Later, the last look, those too were gone.
The trees dripped softly, swaddled in mist,
Raining their lightsome leaves.

250 Night. All dark. All deepness on the land.
All darkness over the shadow-hovered world.

THE BLOWING OF THE SEED

THE SPHYNX

All day my mind has fixed upon your face
That drew me in the dance and was alone
Saddened with a sorrow of its own;
And round that carven image wreathed a wraith
5 As rain is wreathed around the graven stone.

Our years between us like twin rivers ran.
The dance you danced was on a nether shore;
Our bodies gestured but could do no more;
Like mutes we looked across that double span;
10 The years drew out their desultory roar.

Now in the dance's afterbeat I tread
Stiff with constraint, and shuffle out its pace.
The sandy rivers merge about your face,
As round the monolith the rampant dead
15 Drain to their dim and unrevealing place.

I

I speak,
Who am come down from a glacial region north of here,
Where a cold river
Cuts its way to a colder sea,
20 Leaves the brown stain of its mark
Far out, it is said, for the feeding fish.

I speak, I speak.
I speak from the chattering lips of a cold man,
A man cut to the core;
25 Speak from the numbed mouth,
Blue in its dearth;
Speak from the hobbling frame,
From the limp of a cold place,
A cold region.

30 I speak from a cold heart.
I cry out of a cold climate.
I shake the head of a cold-encrusted man.
I blow a blue breath.

I come from a cold place.
35 I cry out for another future.

II
Darkheaded,
And of the olive flesh,
Your arm, in its encirclement,
Like the pure prevailing wind,
40 Blowing for miles from its deep equatorial zone,
Blows to the center of my self,
Thaws.

You of the wide south,
Chinook,
45 Wind of the containing warmth,
Did you know, in your entrance,
What a breath you blew through a heart's dungeon,
Set wide the cells,
The numbed prisoner
50 Agape in his rust,
In his ruin.

When you loosed that look,
That leaping,
A long way off to lay its mark,
55 Like sun on snow,
On the bitter places,

Did you know how it hit,
What broke in your coming,
And what you set free?

III

60 When the rains came over they wetted the forest,
The open slides of the granite peaks,
And the little thickets.

They wetted the salmonberry and the leafless vine;
They wetted the rough trunks of the prone trees
65 Where the treefrog creaked in the branches;
They wetted the place where the hermit hunched,
Fumbling his thumb.

The owl,
In the tamarack,
70 Whoopson, whits.

The mouse,
In the leaden glade,
Gnaws, scuttles.

There is left in that place a little ashes,
75 The butt-end of sticks and the blackened rocks.
There is left in that place only the small leavings of a frugal life,
Too tiny for the swart junket
That skits in the thicket.

There is left in that place
80 Only the smell of a little smoke,
And a little ashes.

IV

If you were to try to say,
Half-closing your eyes in the way you have,
Your mouth pulled in a bit in its pre-speech purpose . . .

85 If you were to turn your face to me,
That sudden look of inward revelation,
When out of so much of thought, so much of thinking—
Out of your nights, as you lie abed and pick up the pieces;
Out of your days;
90 Over whatever task it is you are doing, in whatever place,
Going about your unguessable business
With that air of half-abstraction,
Half-involvement . . .

If you were to lift up your face,
95 And from so dense a demand, so deep a denial;
From your hemmed and hampered past,
When your world was weak,
And all your instance
Turned on the tremble of a touch,
100 And you had no grip, no grasp . . .

If you were to break,
The tears beat from your eyes,
All your hard hurt broke open and bared
In its sudden gust of bleak exposure . . .

105 If you were to try . . .

Under my hand your heart hits like a bird's
Hushed in the palms, a muffled flutter,
And all the instinct of its flight
Shut in its wings.

V

110 And then that humming,
In the tenseness under the skin,
Where the little nerves
Mesh, merge:
In that fabric, that suture,
115 Where there runs out his rapid dance
And pain poises—

There, There.

Under those roots the running of it
Wakens a wind to skirl in the grasses,
120 A rain-dance of wind;
A long passion forming out of its farther region;
A past of such pain,
Of such deprivation;
Out of such hunted hope when none could be had,
125 But yet the hope, the hunger;
Out of such starting
That wind widens,
That wind weaves.

Cry out, cry out,
130 Speak from the bloodied past, the failured venture;
Speak from the broken vows, and the shattered pledges;
Speak from the ruined marriage of flesh
Where joy danced and was denied,
And the harsh croppage of time
135 Reaped its rue in those dolorous arches.

Dance. Dance.
Dance out the troubled dream;
Dance out the murderous pain,
The mutilated silence.
140 Dance out the heart in its narrow hole
Caught in the clamp of that brittle hunger.

Dance in the rags of an old remorse,
In the tattered garments of trust,
Ripped from the narrow thighs,
145 Thrown to the crickets.
Dance and be spent,
Fall in the long gasp,
The heart too hurt, the spirit
Cut too quick—

150 All gone, all broken,
Smashed and smithereened,
And none to know, ever,
None to heed.

Be through with it then,
155 Be finished.
Close out and complete.
Look. I am come.
Like a whirlwind
Mounting out of a foaming sea;
160 I suck all inward.
I shriek.

Dance! Dance!
Dance out the sad bereavement of flesh,
The broken suture.
165 Dance out the weight of the prone years.
Dance out denial.
Dance it out in the heave of that hope,
Sprung from the proud immortal flesh
That shoots up its flower.
170 Dance out the sharp damnation of time
That sets the crowsfeet
Crafty under the blear eye
And has its instance.
Dance it out, all,
175 And be brought low,
And be low broken,
And be brinked.

Now in a black time I come to you
Crouched in your corner of hut by your meager blaze.
180 Now like a man out of a madded dream
I come from my cleavage.
I come running across the flints and notches of a glacial year.
I bear brash on my back.
I wear an old woe.

185 Be joined.
Be clipped.
Be crouched and crotched,
Woman, woman.

Bring me that moaning mouth: I stop it.
190 Bring me the knock of that hurt-empacted heart:
I grind it out.

I level.
I level the last of my life in your life.
I hammer harsher than hooves.
195 I gnaw like knives.

Give me that past and that pain-proud flesh.
I come with the hurled and howling North:
A mad naked man.

VI

Of such touch given;
200 Of such sight—
Your eyes, where the warmth lives on from a late loving,
And your palms,
Placed—

Speak you?

205 That word wears out the woe of the world.

But now as your mouth on it shapes for its sound,
As a sign,
As of some sign given
Long ago, between man, between woman,
210 So on your lip it loudens,
Through those chambers of the mind
Where all past in its slumber
Lives on, lives on.

You speak.

215 And the chimes,
The bronze bells of those death-departed years,
Are all awakened.

EPILOGUE IN A MILD WINTER, FROM THE COAST COUNTRY
Woman, I sing to you now from a new season.
I sing from the freshened creeks,
220 From the Autumn's waning.
I sing where the wind runs in from a wide sea,
Wakens these winter-wet fields to new growth,
A new greening.
I sing from a fallow year that has since been broken;
225 From a drought, a year that has died,
Gone down into deadness.
Known now of your mouth, known of your healing hand,
I sing to you from a richening joy,
A ripening gladness.

230 I sing to you from the spacious river of love
That flows in me now to its sea
With its mild murmur.
I sing from the little leaf that lurks in the bough;
The winter bud that has its hope
235 And will find its summer.

I sing from the barley germinal in the rich acre,
That will sprout and break in time
From its winter mantle.

As in me now the quickening self puts forth,
240 Uncouth, come with my head unkempt,
But my hand gentle.

I sing. I have been fulfilled in a winter season,
Wakened under a rain;
Like the seed of the mustard,
245 Like the seed of the vetch that is harrowed into the hill;
Rolled in the mulch of the lifeless slope,
In the leafless orchard.

I move to meet you now in a greening time.
I come with wind and with wet
250 In a soft season.
I bring you my hand.
I bring you the flesh of those fallow, fallen years;
And my manifest reasons.

A CANTICLE TO THE WATERBIRDS

WRITTEN FOR THE FEAST OF SAINT FRANCIS OF ASSISI, 1950

Clack your beaks you cormorants and kittiwakes,
North on those rock-croppings finger-jutted into the rough Pacific surge;
You migratory terns and pipers who leave but the temporal clawtrack
                    written on sandbars there of your presence;
Grebes and pelicans; you comber-picking scoters and you shorelong gulls;
5 All you keepers of the coastline north of here to the Mendocino beaches;
All you beyond the cliff-face thwarting the surf at Hecate Head;
Hovering the under-surge where the cold Columbia grapples at the bar;
North yet to the Sound, whose islands float like a sown flurry of chips
                    upon the sea:
Break wide your harsh and salt-encrusted beaks unmade for song
10 And say a praise up to the Lord.

And you freshwater egrets east in the flooded marshlands skirting the sea-
     level rivers, white one-legged watchers of shallows;
Broad-headed kingfishers minnow-hunting from willow stems on meander-
     ing valley sloughs;
You too, you herons, blue and supple-throated, stately, taking the air
     majestical in the sunflooded San Joaquin,
Grading down on your belted wings from the upper lights of sunset,
15 Mating over the willow clumps or where the flatwater rice fields shimmer;
You killdeer, high night-criers, far in the moon-suffusion sky;
Bitterns, sand-waders, all shore-walkers, all roost-keepers,
Populates of the 'dobe cliffs of the Sacramento:
Open your water-dartling beaks,
20 And make a praise up to the Lord.

For you hold the heart of His mighty fastnesses,
And shape the life of His indeterminate realms.
You are everywhere on the lonesome shores of His wide creation.
You keep seclusion where no man may go, giving Him praise;
25 Nor may a woman come to lift like your cleaving flight her clear con-
     tralto song
To honor the spindrift gifts of His soft abundance.
You sanctify His hermitage rocks where no holy priest may kneel to adore,
     no holy nun assist;
And where his true communion-keepers are not enabled to enter.

And well may you say His praises, birds, for your ways
30 Are verved with the secret skills of His inclinations,
And your habits plaited and rare with the subdued elaboration of His
     intricate craft;
Your days intent with the direct astuteness needful for His outworking,
And your nights alive with the dense repose of His infinite sleep.
You are His secretive charges and you serve His secretive ends,
35 In His clouded mist-conditioned stations, in His murk,
Obscure in your matted nestings, immured in His limitless ranges.
He makes you penetrate through dark interstitial joinings of His thicketed
     kingdoms,
And keep your concourse in the deeps of His shadowed world.

Your ways are wild but earnest, your manners grave,
40 Your customs carefully schooled to the note of His serious mien.

You hold the prime conditions of His clean creating,
And the swift compliance with which you serve His minor means
Speaks of the constancy with which you hold Him.
For what is your high flight forever going home to your first beginnings,
45 But such a testament to your devotion?
You hold His outstretched world beneath your wings, and mount upon
His storms,
And keep your sheer wind-lidded sight upon the vast perspectives of His
mazy latitudes.

But mostly it is your way you bear existence wholly within the context of
His utter will and are untroubled.
Day upon day you do not reckon, nor scrutinize tomorrow, nor multiply
the nightfalls with a rash concern,
50 But rather assume each instant as warrant sufficient of His final seal.
Wholly in Providence you spring, and when you die you look on death
in clarity unflinched,
Go down, a clutch of feather ragged upon the brush;
Or drop on water where you briefly lived, found food,
And now yourselves made food for His deep current-keeping fish, and
then are gone:
55 Is left but the pinion-feather spinning a bit on the uproil
Where lately the dorsal cut clear air.

You leave a silence. And this for you suffices, who are not of the cere-
monials of man,
And hence are not made sad to now forgo them.
Yours is of another order of being, and wholly it compels.
60 But may you, birds, utterly seized in God's supremacy,
Austerely living under his austere eye—
Yet may you teach a man a necessary thing to know,
Which has to do of the strict conformity that creaturehood entails,
And constitutes the prime commitment all things share.
65 For God has given you the imponderable grace to *be* His verification,
Outside the mulled incertitude of our forensic choices;
That you, our lessers in the rich hegemony of Being,
May serve as testament to what a creature is,
And what creation owes.

70 Curlews, stilts and scissortails, beachcomber gulls,
Wave-haunters, shore-keepers, rockhead-holders, all cape-top vigilantes,
Now give God praise.
Send up the articulation of your throats,
And say His name.

THE MAKING OF THE CROSS

Rough fir, hauled from the hills. And the tree it had been,
Lithe-limbed, wherein the wren had nested,
Whereon the red hawk and the grey
Rested from flight, and the raw-head vulture
5 Shouldered to his feed—that tree went over
Bladed down with a double-bitted axe; was snaked with winches;
The wedge split it; hewn with the adze
It lay to season toward its use.

So too with the nails: milleniums under the earth,
10 Pure ore; chunked out with picks; the nail-shape
Struck in the pelt-lunged forge; tonged to a cask
And the wait against that work.

Even the thorn-bush flourished from afar,
As do the flourishing generations of its kind,
15 Filling the shallow soil no one wants;
Wind-sown, it cuts the cattle and the wild horse;
It tears the cloth of man, and hurts his hand.

Just as in life the good things of the earth
Are patiently assembled: some from here, some from there;
20 Wine from the hill and wheat from the valley;
Rain that comes blue-bellied out of the sopping sea;
Snow that keeps its drift on the gooseberry ridge,
Will melt with May, go down, take the egg of the salmon,
Serve the traffic of otters and fishes,
25 Be ditched to orchards . . .

So too are gathered up the possibles of evil.

And when the Cross was joined, quartered,
As is the earth; spoked, as is the Universal Wheel—
Those radials that led all unregenerate act
30 Inward to innocence—it met the thorn-wove Crown;
It found the Scourges and the Dice;
The Nail was given and the reed-lifted Sponge;
The Curse caught forward out of the heart corrupt;
The excoriate Foul, stoned with the thunder and the hail—
35 All these made up that miscellaneous wrath
And were assumed.

The evil and the wastage and the woe,
As if the earth's old cyst, back down the slough
To Adam's sin-burnt calcinated bones
40 Rushed out of time and clotted on the Cross.

Off there the cougar
Coughed in passion when the sun went out; the rattler
Filmed his glinty eye, and found his hole.

PASSION WEEK

Christ-cut: the cedar
Bleeds where I gashed it.

Lance wound under the narrow rib.

Eve's orifice: the agony of Abel
5 Enacted out on the Tree.

Blood gushed
From the gash.

The Holy Ghost
Gusted out of the sky
10 Aghast.

Our Guest.

Bleed cedar.
Little cedar,
Lanced,
15 Axe-opened,
The ache of sacrifice.

Pour out,
As Christ,
Those pearls of pain,
20 Bequeathed.

O bleed
Little cedar,
Bleed for the blooded Heart,
For the pang of man . . .

25 The earth's
Old ache.

THE POET IS DEAD

A MEMORIAL FOR ROBINSON JEFFERS

To be read with a full stop between the strophes, as in a dirge.

In the evening the dusk
Stipples with lights. The long shore
Gathers darkness in on itself
And goes cold. From the lap of silence
5 All the tide-crest's pivotal immensity
Lifts into the land.

The great tongue is dried.
The teeth that bit to the bitterness
Are sheathed in truth.

10 For the poet is dead.
The pen, splintered on the sheer
Excesses of vision, unfingered, falls.
The heart-crookt hand, cold as a stone,
Lets it go down.

15 If you listen
You can hear the field mice
Kick little spurts in the grasses.
You can hear
Time take back its own.

20 For the poet is dead.
On the bed by the window,
Where dislike and desire
Killed each other in the crystalline interest,
What remains alone lets go of its light. It has found
25 Finalness. It has touched what it craved: the passionate
Darks of deliverance.

At sundown the sea wind,
Burgeoning,
Bled the west empty.

30 Now the opulent
Treacherous woman called Life
Forsakes her claim. Blond and a harlot
She once drank joy from his narrow loins.
She broke his virtue in her knees.

35 In the water-gnawn coves of Point Lobos
The white-faced sea otters
Fold their paws on their velvet breasts
And list waveward.

But he healed his pain on the wisdom of stone,
40 He touched roots for his peace.

The old ocean boils its wrack,
It steeps its lees.

For the poet is dead. The gaunt wolf
Crawled out to the edge and died snapping.
45 He said he would. The wolf
Who lost his mate. He said he would carry the wound,
The blood-wound of life, to the broken edge
And die grinning.

Over the salt marsh the killdeer,
50 Unrestrainable,
Cry fear against moon set.

And all the hardly suspected
Latencies of disintegration
Inch forward. The skin
55 Flakes loss. On the death-gripped feet
The toenails glint like eyeteeth
From the pinched flesh.
The caged ribs and the bladed shoulders,
Ancient slopes of containment,
60 Imperceptibly define the shelves of structure,
Faced like rock ridges
Boned out of mountains, absently revealed
With the going of the snow.

In the sleeve of darkness the gopher
65 Tunnels the sod for short grass
And pockets his fill.

And the great phallus shrinks in the groin,
The seed in the scrotum
Chills.

70 When the dawn comes in again,
Thoughtlessly,
The sea birds will mew by the window.

For the poet is dead. Beyond the courtyard
The ocean at full tide hunches its bulk.
75 Groping among the out-thrusts of granite
It moans and whimpers. In the phosphorescent
Restlessness it chunks deceptively,
Wagging its torn appendages, dipping and rinsing
Its ripped sea rags, its strip-weeded kelp.
80 The old mother grieves her deathling.
She trundles the dark for her lost child.
She hunts her son.

On the top of the tower
The hawk will not perch tomorrow.

85 But in the gorged rivermouth
Already the steelhead fight for entry.
They feel fresh water
Sting through the sieves of their salt-coarsened gills.
They shudder and thrust.

90 So the sea broods. And the aged gull,
Asleep on the water, too stiff to feed,
Spins in a side-rip crossing the surf
And drags down.

This mouth is shut. I say
95 The mouth is clamped cold.
I tell you this tongue is dried.

But the skull, the skull,
The perfect sculpture of bone!—
Around the forehead the fine hair,
100 Composed to the severest
Lineaments of thought,
Is moulded on peace.

And the strongly wrought features,
That keep in the soul's serenest achievement
105 The spirit's virtue,
Set the death mask of all mortality,
The impress of that grace.

In the shoal-champed breakers
One wing of the gull
110 Tilts like a fin through the ribbon of spume
And knifes under.

And all about there the vastness of night
Affirms its sovereignty. There's not a cliff
Of the coastline, not a reef
115 Of the waterways, from the sword-thrust Aleutians
To the scorpion-tailed stinger Cape Horn—
All that staggering declivity
Grasped in the visionary mind and established—
But is sunken under the dark ordainment,
120 Like a sleeper possessed, like a man
Gone under, like a powerful swimmer
Plunged in a womb-death washed out to sea
And worked back ashore.

The gull's eye,
125 Skinned to the wave, retains the ocean's
Imponderable compression,
And burns yellow.

The poet is dead. I tell you
The nostrils are narrowed. I say again and again
130 The strong tongue is broken.

But the owl
Quirks in the cypresses, and you hear
What he says. He is calling for something.
He tucks his head for his mate's
135 Immemorial whisper. In her answering voice
He tastes the grace-note of his reprieve.

If there is fog in the canyons
The redwoods will know what it means.
The giant sisters
140 Gather it into their merciful arms
And stroke silence.

When you smell pine resin laced in the salt
You know the dawn wind has veered.

And on the shelf in the gloom,
145 Blended together, the tall books emerge,
All of a piece. Transparent as membranes
The thin leaves of paper hug their dark thoughts.
They know what he said.

The sea, reaching for life,
150 Spits up the gull. He falls spread-eagled,
The streaked wings swept on the sand.
When the blind head snaps
The beak krakes at the sky.

Now the night closes.
155 All the dark's negatory
Decentralization
Quivers toward dawn.

He has gone into death like a stone thrown in the sea.

And in far places the morning
160 Shrills its episodes of triviality and vice
And one man's passing. Could the ears
That hardly listened in life
Care much less now?

The great tongue
165 Dries in the mouth. I told you.
The voiceless throat
Cools silence. And the sea-granite eyes.
Washed in the sibilant waters
The stretched lips kiss peace.

170 The poet is dead.

Nor will ever again hear the sea lions
Grunt in the kelp at Point Lobos.
Nor look to the south when the grunion
Run the Pacific, and the plunging
175 Shearwaters, insatiable,
Stun themselves in the sea.

THE SOUTH COAST

Salt creek mouths unflushed by the sea
And the long day shuts down.
Whose hand stacks rock, cairn-posted,
Churched to the folded sole of this hill,
5 And Whose mind conceives? Three herons
Gig their necks in the tule brake
And the prying mudhen plies.

Long down, far south to Sur, the wind lags,
Slosh-washes his slow heel,
10 Lays off our coast, rump of the domed
Mountain, woman-backed, bedded
Under his lea. Slat grasses here,
Fringes, twigging the crevice slips,
And the gagging cypress
15 Wracked away from the sea.
God *makes*. On earth, in us, most instantly,
On the very now,
His own means conceives.
How many strengths break out unchoked
20 Where He, Whom all declares,
Delights to make be!

from A FROST LAY WHITE ON CALIFORNIA
. . .

Was this a dream,
Some phantasy of anguish?
I crouched in my stall all night.
It was winter, midwinter.
5 A frost lay white on California.
I felt stars crack blue in my brain.

*"I ask nothing of you," cried God, "that you wouldn't accord a dog!
I told you that!
The sheerest recognition.
10 That I do exist.
That I am yours.
Close your eyes now and be what I am.
Which is—yourself!
The you who am I!"*

15 The roof of the chapel split up the sky,
A tree-wedge in a stump.
I felt the cold stitch my bones.
I should be in bed.

This is a fool to knock about here in the frozen hour,
20 Champing my teeth like a chittering ghost.
Who do I think I am?

"Who, indeed," cried God, "when you think what you think?
Ask me who, I will tell it!
How far do I have to go?
25 Look! I crawl at your feet!
I, the God-dog!
I am all woman!
I eat from your hand!
Feed me. All I ask is your heart.
30 Am I that ugly?"

The light woke in the windows.
One by one the saints existed,
The swords of their martyrdom healed in their hands.
The linnet opened his voice;
35 He blistered his throat on the seethe of that rapture.
The suddenness split my skull.

"No pride!" cried God, "kick me I come back!
Spit on me I eat your spittle!
I crawl on my belly!
40 What is revulsion to me?
As free of disgust as of shame and pride.
As much your dog as I am your God.
Whatever you need.
When you have gutted this madness
45 Drop down on the ground.
I will lick your hand."

That was the moment the dawn dragged in,
The cloud closed. It had slid from the sea,
Almost a sneak. I stood up in my stall,
50 Flung off my cloak. I heard the rain begin.

It was falling on the roof,
A slow spilth of deliverance,
Falling far, very far.

It was falling, I knew, out of the terrifying helplessness of God.

55 Into the frost,
Into the frozen crotches of the bush,
Into the feather of the singing bird.

Across the stuttering mouths of those seeds;
Against the sob of my tongue.

IN ALL THESE ACTS

Cleave the wood and thou shalt find Me,
lift the rock and I am there!
        —The Gospel According to Thomas

Dawn cried out: the brutal voice of a bird
Flattened the seaglaze. Treading that surf
Hunch-headed fishers toed small agates,
Their delicate legs, iridescent, stilting the ripples.
5 Suddenly the cloud closed. They heard the big wind
Boom back on the cliff, crunch timber over along the ridge.
They shook up their wings, crying; terror flustered their pinions.
Then hemlock, tall, torn by the roots, went crazily down,
The staggering gyrations of splintered kindling.
10 Flung out of bracken, fleet mule deer bolted;
But the great elk, caught midway between two scissoring logs,
Arched belly-up and died, the snapped spine
Half torn out of his peeled back, his hind legs
Jerking that gasped convulsion, the kick of spasmed life,
15 Paunch plowed open, purple entrails
Disgorged from the basketwork ribs
Erupting out, splashed sideways, wrapping him,
Gouted in blood, flecked with the brittle sliver of bone.

Frenzied, the terrible head
20 Thrashed off its antlered fuzz in that rubble
And then fell still, the great tongue
That had bugled in rut, calling the cow-elk up from the glades,
Thrust agonized out, the maimed member
Bloodily stiff in the stone-smashed teeth . . .

                          Far down below,
25 The mountain torrent, that once having started
Could never be stopped, scooped up that avalanchial wrack
And strung it along, a riddle of bubble and littered duff
Spun down its thread. At the gorged river mouth
The sea plunged violently in, gasping its potholes,
30 Sucked and panted, answering itself in its spume.
The river, spent at last, beating driftwood up and down
In a frenzy of capitulation, pumped out its life,
Destroying itself in the mother sea,
There where the mammoth sea-grown salmon
35 Lurk immemorial, roe in their hulls, about to begin.
They will beat that barbarous beauty out
On those high-stacked shallows, those headwater claims,
Back where they were born. Along that upward-racing trek
Time springs through all its loops and flanges,
40 The many-faced splendor and the music of the leaf,
The copulation of beasts and the watery laughter of drakes,
Too few the grave witnesses, the wakeful, vengeful beauty,
Devolving itself of its whole constraint,
Erupting as it goes.

              In all these acts
45 Christ crouches and seethes, pitched forward
On the crucifying stroke, juvescent, that will spring Him
Out of the germ, out of the belly of the dying buck,
Out of the father-phallus and the torn-up root.
These are the modes of His forth-showing,
50 His serene agonization. In the clicking teeth of otters
Over and over He dies and is born,
Shaping the weasel's jaw in His leap
And the staggering rush of the bass.

THE KISS OF THE CROSS

I

I cry.

Once of this world,
Woman of God,
What do you betoken?

5 Heart of fire,
Violence of flesh,
The spirit's flash,
Voice of tolled desire.

Tongue of wrath,
10 Latencies, the fierce
Evocation: semblances,
The shut darkness broken.

Over the bay
City-light wavers and spurns.
15 One steamer
Sidles the mist,
Homes the black harbor.

Pound heart,
Heart of the splendored rapture,
20 Ruptured on death.

In the trace of a hand,
On the mystery of a face
The brute heart is shaken.

II

The heart reaves: my flesh
25 Coughs from its clotted need,
One flex of possession.

All flung pride
Crashes on that crest.

Her face reels,
30 God's voice blares.

The crucifix
Snaps.

In the tongs of passion
Is torn,
35 Is torn.

Let the heart be hit
If ever it can.
Let the bludgeoned soul
Stone its mute mouth.

40 In the outreach of love,
In the passion of possession,
I nailed my desire.

III

Heart be hushed.
Let it howk and then hush.

45 Let the black wave break.
Let the terrible tongue
Engorge my deeps.

Let the loins of ferocity
Lave my shut flesh.

50 I killed the Christ.

On the inch of my pride,
On the diamond of my desire,
In the pierce of a woman's goodness,
By the token of her grace.

55 I who crept toward him year after year
Murdered my God.

IV

I crept.

I brought Him gifts,
Hushed in my heart.

60 I brought what I had.

I crept.

I gave Him every gift of myself.
I brought Him all the wholeness I had.

V

I brought Him my wholeness,
65 That wholeness was split.

I brought Him my burden,
That burden broke.

I brought Him my all,
My all was empty.

70 In the wrath of flesh
I heard His bone
Snap like a nerve.

My passion poured.

VI

My passion poured.

75 I heard his nerve
Snap like a bone.

I came:
        up out of darkness,
        deep holes and recesses,
80   black wells and cisterns of the self—
    I came!
    I came!

    I cried my pang!
    The burden
85 Split bone in the dark!

    He shrieked.

    As I gasped
    He fell dead.

    I panted across her face
90 Feeling Him bleed.

    I saw her kneel.
    She kissed His cross.

    VII
    She kissed.
    My shame charred my face.
95 With her voice she consoled.
    In her mother-hands
    She knitted His bones.

    When she kissed His knees
    His face smiled.

100 I thrashed in that dark
    Strangled with guilt.

    What deeds of wrath from the split gift!

    Shameful the face of the shocked man
    Who wept in my place.

105 I spit heart's blood.
My fist a claw scrabbled my heart.

She kissed.
I saw Him sag.

That dark was dead.

VIII
110 She kissed.

With her lips she consoled.
My soul shook.

I screeched back in dread.

As a cool water flows
115 Her words were.

I saw stars steeped in death over San Francisco.

Her words:
She gave up a song that a heart might heal.
I flinched on her prayer.

120 Picking my sin like a stone out of dirt
I bore it home.

I held it against my raddled groin
My jewel of pain on which Christ died.

While I slept it burned on.

IX
125 While I slept it burned.
A stone in my bed it lay nightlong,
A passion to purge me.

In my mirror of death
Her face sustained me.

130 In my substance of guilt
Her purity betrayed me.

I slashed with my seed.

She bore the flesh-wound under the breast,
The mother-burden.

135 By the kissed cross,
Where the Christ-nerve
Snapped when my passion poured.
Clinched on the Tree:

She brought me back.

X

140 She brought me back,
The kiss that kept me:

A heart to heal,
A death to die,
The debt of a death.

145 I was brought back alive.

Drenched in that deed when passion poured,
Her purity betrayed me.

Merciless that armor
Turned the point of my brutal tongue.

150 I fell stunned.

She picked up the pieces.
One by one she put them together.
Piece by piece she made a whole.

She brought back a man.

XI

155 Cross-kissed I stagger.

Her face that broke the harbor's beauty
Revokes my passion.

A graciousness redeems.

In the purity of touch,
160 On the trace of a selfless passion,

Athwart the trajectory of an ancient lust,
I signed a saint.

Her lips, her lips, the mystery of a perfect face!

She bowed her head when Christ broke.
165 As I wept she smiled.

In the innocence of little children
Her wisdom wells:

My choked desire.

XII

O Christ & Lady
170 Save me from my law!

O Christ & Lady
Save me from my seed!

O Christ & Lady
Save me from my tongue!

175 O Christ & Lady
Save me from my curse!

O Christ & Lady
Save me from my moan!

O Christ & Lady
180 O Christ & Lady
Save me from myself!

XIII

Let no woe be spoken.

Wake not a word.
No haplessness unearth
185 From any deepness broken.

A timelessness of pain,
An endlessness of love,
The mystery of person.

Redeemed, restored,
190 She verifies my token:

God is not gone.
Christ is not cold.
The Wound will not worsen.

THE UNDERLYING TORSION

A lull of no wind.
And out of the ashen
Death-drugged sky
A drizzle for thaw,
5 A feathery drift: the vague
Fingers of life-reviving quest
Tracing the snow.

Over the beech forests,
Over the hickory woods and the sap maple thickets
10 That did freeze in the awful zero of cold:
The slow lease of nascent relaxation,
A soft uncramping.

And I think of the svelte
Hills of California, their lambent nudeness,
15 Prone on the shore beside the dalliance of beaches,
Redisposing in their immemorial womanly way
The underlying torsion of earth's old flaw,
The lock-jawed lips of the San Andreas fault.

And here, far away, in the frozen
20 Core of New England,
Ice in the veins of the Puritan heart,
I hear the snow
Slip from the branches,
And bring back to my mind
25 The subtropical presence,
The death-dissolving movement in wisdom and in warmth,
Of one out there
Who laughs her way through the spring-haunted glades,
Bestowing on all whom she touches,
30 Given out of her maiden-heart and her mother-eyes,
God's gaze, God's liberating look.

from THE FACE I KNOW

And I crawl.
I will get there.
Like a clubbed snake
I hitch toward freedom.
5 Out of this skin, this slough,
Across these illusions,
Upon this blood.

No law
But the law of deprivation.

10 No hope
But the hope of deliverance.

No curse
But the curse of the uncaptived.

from THE RAGING OF THE ROSE

Two egos, Selfed in unison, moded on the subsistence of Christ,
His single Isness.
She taught me: how one is free,
Possessing freedom in subsistence,
5 What freedom is.
I taught her: how the crest of emotion,
That freedom,
Is crowned on the undersurge of intellectual passion,
Which is depth.

10 She taught me: what deliverance is,
The freedom that is salvation.
In truth, in truth,
That the free
Is freedom as truth
15 Is being,
The crest of release
That liberates freedom
In the primacy of response,
The *act* of existence.

20 As act, being: His *esse:* to be.

So she: I.
In us: He is.
We Three
Free.

The Poems in Chronological Order of Appearance in Generally Available Editions

Poems from THE RESIDUAL YEARS, 1948

LAVA BED
THE RAID
LET BREATH KEEP TO THE LUNG
LINES FOR THE LAST OF A GOLD TOWN
NOON
WALLS
THE STRANGER
THE ANSWER
THE FRIENDS
THE ILLUSION
THE HARE: AN EARLIER EPISODE
THE RESIDUAL YEARS
THE OUTLAW
THE REVOLUTIONIST
THE UNKILLABLE KNOWLEDGE
THE APPROACH
THE VOW
from CHRONICLE OF DIVISION

Poems from THE CROOKED LINES OF GOD, 1960

A CANTICLE TO THE WATERBIRDS
THE MAKING OF THE CROSS
THE SOUTH COAST

Poems from THE HAZARDS OF HOLINESS, 1962

PASSION WEEK
from A FROST LAY WHITE ON CALIFORNIA
IN ALL THESE ACTS

THE POET IS DEAD, 1964

Poems from SINGLE SOURCE, 1966

OUTSIDE THIS MUSIC
TRIFLES
ON THE ANNIVERSARY OF THE VERSAILLES PEACE, 1936
CIRCUMSTANCE

THE BLOWING OF THE SEED, 1966

Poems from THE ROSE OF SOLITUDE, 1967

THE KISS OF THE CROSS
THE UNDERLYING TORSION
from THE FACE I KNOW
from THE RAGING OF THE ROSE

from THE SPRINGING OF THE BLADE, 1967

INDEX OF FIRST LINES AND TITLES

1 2 3 4 5 6 7 8 9 10 11 12 13 14 15 16 17 18 19 20 21 22 23 24 25 SH 74 73 72 71 70 69 68 67